W9-AJN-314

ICE ROAD TRUCKERS
IN ACTION

BY AMY C. REA

The Child's World®
childsworld.com

Published by The Child's World®
1980 Lookout Drive • Mankato, MN 56003-1705
800-599-READ • www.childsworld.com

Photographs ©: Matthew Porter/iStockphoto, cover; Shutterstock Images,
5, 10, 27; Stephen Mcsweeny/Shutterstock Images, 6; Glynnis Jones/
Shutterstock Images, 9; Eugene Sergeev/Shutterstock Images, 12; Vander
Wolf Images/Dreamstime, 14; Vereshchagin Dmitry/Shutterstock Images,
15; Lisa McDonald/iStockphoto, 16; Robert Carner/iStockphoto, 18; Sergei
Karpukhin/Dreamstime, 21, 22; R. Stapleton/Alaska Journal of Commerce/AP
Images, 24; Neil Burton/Shutterstock Images, 28

ISBN 9781503816305

LCCN 2016945861

Printed in the United States of America
PA02320

TABLE OF
CONTENTS

FAST FACTS

What's the Job?

- Ice road truckers drive large trucks over roads made of ice. They go over frozen bodies of water to remote parts of Alaska and northern Canada.
- Truck drivers should have at least five years of trucking experience.
- The trucking companies provide additional training. Mechanical experience is helpful.

The Dangers

- It is difficult to know whether an ice road is safe to drive on.
- Air temperatures can be as cold as −40 degrees Fahrenheit (−40°C), which is very dangerous. The water under the ice is cold enough to kill a person very quickly.
- Ice conditions can change quickly, making a previously safe road unsafe.
- Snowstorms can cause drivers to go off the ice road onto thinner, less-safe ice.
- Wild animals are present, including predators such as wolves and polar bears.

Important Stats

- Ice road truckers can earn anywhere from $20,000 to $80,000 in a single season. The amount drivers earn depends on how long the season is, how many runs they make, and their experience level.

- High turnover means freight companies are always looking for new drivers each season.

Chapter 1

BUILDING AN ICE ROAD

In northern Canada, the first ice formed in November. The worker got ready to build ice roads. He knew this was a serious job. It was his responsibility to make sure the ice roads were safe. But he knew that building the road could be very dangerous.

Even though people called them "ice roads," the worker knew they were not really roads. A typical road is built on land. Ice roads are built on water. The ice roads cross rivers, swamps, and lakes. For that to work, the water they cross must be frozen. That means ice roads can be built only in the winter. And the roads last for only one season before they melt.

The ice road worker put on a bright orange survival suit. He knew this suit would help him float if he broke through the ice. He could not begin work on the road without it. The worker was also glad to be using a lightweight **amphibious** vehicle. The vehicle had wheels, but it could also float. This made driving on the ice much safer. A regular truck would sink if the ice broke beneath it.

◀ Augers are important tools for the people who build ice roads.

But with the amphibious vehicle, the worker had a better chance of escaping if the ice broke.

The worker still had many things to worry about. The previous winter had been very cold. The low temperatures had helped the ice become thick and solid. This year was different. There had been a lot of snow this year. The snow prevented the ice from becoming as solid as the worker needed it to be. The ice must be very strong to build a road. The worker knew it had to support trucks that weighed up to 70 short tons (64 metric tons). Because of the snow, he could not build the road in the same place as the year before.

Out on the new ice, the worker used hand tools and **augers** to drill a hole in the ice. This drilling helped him figure out how deep the ice was. After many tests, the worker decided on the best location for the ice road that winter. He needed the ice to be at least 1 foot (.3 m) thick before road clearing began.

Once he found the right ice, the worker used a lightweight snowplow called a snowcat to plow the road. He knew that it was important to remove the snow. Snow is an **insulator** that can keep the ice warm and thin. When the worker removed the snow, the cold northern air made the ice stronger and thicker.

A survival suit can keep a worker warm if he or she falls ▶ through the ice.

A couple of weeks later, the ice was 3 feet (.9 m) thick. The worker traded the snowcat for heavier snowplows to keep the roads clear. Once he cleared the new roads, the ice trucks could start delivering products. After the heaviest trucks made a few successful runs, the roads would be open to the public. The worker knew this was important, too. People who could not leave their communities in the summer months could now use the ice roads for a short period of time.

After building ice roads for several years, the worker began to realize that climate change was creating new challenges for ice road truckers. As the planet slowly warms, the winter season is becoming shorter. The worker worried that eventually the ice would not be thick enough to build a road. Then heavy trucks would no longer be able to drive across the ice. The worker started talking to ice road truckers about different types of equipment and trucks that weighed less. He also began experimenting with different ways of setting up driving tracks.

People sometimes asked the worker why there were no permanent, year-round roads in these far-off places. He explained that building an ice road costs about $1 million. Building a permanent road would cost $100 million or more. Keeping the ice roads working is far less expensive.

◄ A snowcat helps clear the snow off an ice road.

Chapter 2

RACING TIME AND TEMPERATURE

Vlad Pleskot knew he was taking a risk. He was making one last run over the ice roads to help a community in need. Spring was coming. For many people, that is a good thing. But for an ice road trucker, spring means the end of the trucking season. It also means a dangerous job can become even more unsafe.

Vlad was driving to a small, remote community in northern Canada. His truck was filled with items needed to maintain a **water treatment plant**. If he did not make the delivery, the community would not have clean water for several months. There was no way to reach the area without the ice roads.

Vlad understood the dangers of living without clean, safe water. But he also knew the dangers of making the last delivery of the season. He needed to cross lakes and rivers where the ice was becoming thinner and thinner.

◀ **Melting ice is a huge danger for ice road truckers.**

▲ **Drivers sometimes have to put their trucks on barges when the water thaws.**

Vlad was not sure if the ice was still strong enough to hold the weight of his truck. But he decided to try to make the trip. It took two days to drive to the delivery spot. At one point, he even had to put his truck on a **barge** to cross a thawing lake. Clearly the ice roads were not going to last much longer.

Vlad was the last ice road trucker doing a delivery this season. If he found himself in trouble, no one else could help him. He could not rely on his cell phone either. The ice road was so far away from towns that cell phones did not work.

Truckers usually rest for a while at their destination. But Vlad was worried about the road conditions. As soon as his truck was unloaded, he turned around and headed home. Instead of a thick layer of ice under his wheels, he began driving on softer, slushier surfaces.

▲ Truckers cannot stop to change their tires when they are on thin ice.

As his truck entered muddy stretches with swamps under the ice, Vlad was in danger of his truck becoming trapped. He could tell the truck had a flat tire. But he knew that if he stopped to fix it, the truck would likely sink. He would not be able to jack it up high enough to change the flat tire. Instead, he would be stuck in the mud. Once stuck, he would not be able to get the truck out until the following winter. By then, the truck would not be usable.

Finally, Vlad reached a patch of ground that was more stable. He got out to look at the tire. Then he found a wooden stick to put into the hole in the tire. The stick would act as a patch.

After pumping up the tire, Vlad continued driving. For 13 hours, he stopped every 30 minutes to put more air into the tire. Finally, he reached paved roads, where he could jack up the truck and change the flat. He still had 800 miles (1,287 km) to go. But for the rest of the journey, he had a fresh tire and paved roads. He no longer had to worry about stranding his truck. It had been a scary drive, but he was happy that it had ended well.

◀ **A jack helps the driver lift the truck when changing a tire.**

Chapter 3

LEARNING TO DRIVE THE ICE ROADS

As winter began, the trucker got ready to drive on the ice road. She knew that the ice road was 3 feet (.9 m) thick. But she never forgot that under the ice was a body of cold, powerful water. She felt the water moving under her truck while she drove. This job was very different from driving on a paved road. The water below the surface was powerful enough to move both the ice and the truck driving on top of it.

Over the years, the trucker learned how the water moved beneath her. She understood how the truck's speed affected the water and ice. She knew that speeding on any road was dangerous, but it was even worse on an ice road.

Even though the ice was thick, the trucker noticed that the weight of the truck made the ice dip down. It acted like a trampoline when someone steps on it.

◀ Ice road truckers risk their lives to deliver goods to isolated communities.

As she felt the road dip, the trucker wondered if the ice would hold. If the ice broke, she and her truck would fall into the water. If that happened, she would have only a few seconds to get out of the truck before it filled with icy water. The driver unbuckled her seat belt so that she could make the fastest possible escape if the ice broke. This ice road was the one place in the world where it was not always safe to use a seat belt.

As the trucker drove on the ice road, the weight of her truck created a wave under the ice. She knew this wave was created by the weight of the truck pushing down on the ice. The ice moved the water underneath it. The trucker looked through her windshield and saw the wave moving ahead of the truck. She wanted to drive faster to get past the wave. But she knew if the truck moved too fast, the wave would build up and could break through the ice.

The trucker also knew that she should not stop on the ice. The weight of the stopped truck could damage the ice. So she had to find the safest speed to keep going. From driving in previous winters, she knew the best speed was about 22 miles per hour (34 km/h). But on this day, the waves were larger than usual. The trucker had to slow down to only 5 miles per hour (8 km/h).

Drivers have to be careful not to go too fast on ice roads. ▶

She had to stay at this speed for several hours. Driving so slowly was very boring. But the trucker could not allow her mind to wander. She had to pay close attention to the wave in front of her truck. If she didn't, she might begin to drive too fast. If that happened, she was in danger of losing control of her truck and colliding with other trucks.

In addition to carefully watching her own speed, the trucker always had to keep a safe distance from other vehicles. The ice could crack if she drove too near another trucker who was going too fast. The faster driver might be able to get across the crack, but the next driver could fall into it.

The trucker had driven the ice roads enough to know that no matter how safely she drove, she could unexpectedly find herself in trouble. There were so many things beyond her control. So she reminded herself to stay constantly aware and drive at the safest speeds to keep her risk as low as possible.

◀ **Truckers cannot get too close to each other on an ice road.**

Chapter 4

WIND, SNOW, AND WILDLIFE

Hugh Rowland set out on a 350-mile (563-km) drive at four o'clock in the morning. He was delivering cement to a mine in northern Canada. He turned on the radio. The station announcer said a snowstorm was coming. Hugh estimated it would take 48 hours for the storm to reach his area. He did some math in his head. He thought he could complete the round-trip drive in 44 hours. That meant he would just miss the storm.

But a few hours into the trip, Hugh came across another driver whose truck had spun out. It took more than four hours to get the stranded truck back onto the road. In the meantime, Hugh had no choice but to wait. The road was blocked.

By the time Hugh could continue his drive, the storm was getting closer. He reached his destination and unloaded his truck. Then he turned back. The storm reached him when he was just a few miles into his return drive. Heavy snow and high winds made his empty truck rock back and forth. The snow fell fast.

◄ **Ice road truckers have to get started before the sun comes up.**

Soon the snow created a **whiteout.** Hugh could not see anything around him. The truck itself would no longer move forward on the snow-covered ice. Hugh was stuck.

When a storm strikes, snowplows go to a route that has lots of drivers first. But Hugh was alone on his route. He knew it would be a very long time before any help arrived. The cold weather made it too dangerous for him to leave his truck. He had no choice but to stay inside. He kept the engine running so he did not freeze to death.

Before long, Hugh had to go to the bathroom. He knew this was dangerous even if he stood right by the truck. On his drives, Hugh had seen wild animals that are predators. Animals such as wolverines, polar bears, and wolves roam these frozen places looking for food. If a truck sits long enough, wolverines will even make a den under the truck. Then, when a driver tries to step out of the truck, the wolverine attacks. Hugh had been attacked once before. He knew he had to be careful when he opened the door. Luckily, this time there were no predators near or under his truck. He was safe.

It took 36 hours before a snowplow reached Hugh's location. The snowplow dug him out and got him back on the road again.

A winter storm can make it difficult for drivers to see ▶
the road.

Hugh returned to his base. Then he filled his truck with freight and went out on another delivery.

For ice road truckers, the goal is to deliver as much freight as possible during the season. That means they keep going, even after a scary experience.

THINK ABOUT IT

- What are some of the dangers of ice road trucking? Can you think of any ways to make this job safer?
- What kind of person would make a good ice road trucker? Do you think you have what it takes to succeed at this job?
- Would you want to be an ice road trucker? What part of the job would you enjoy the most? What part would you enjoy the least?
- Ice road trucking has a high rate of turnover. That means drivers often quit. Why do you think this happens?

◄ Wolverines can be extremely dangerous.

GLOSSARY

amphibious (am-FIB-ee-us): Amphibious means able to be used on both land and water. The worker drove the amphibious vehicle from a lake to a road.

augers (AW-gerz): Augers are sharp tools used for making holes. The ice road builder used an auger to check the thickness of the ice.

barge (BARJ): A barge is a large, flat-bottomed boat used to carry freight on waterways. The barge towed supplies up the river.

insulator (IN-suh-lay-tur): An insulator is a material that traps heat or cold. Snow is an insulator because it keeps the ice below it warm.

water treatment plant (WAH-ter TREET-ment PLANT): A water treatment plant makes water safe for humans to use. Most cities have a water treatment plant to make sure people have safe water to drink.

whiteout (WITE-out): A whiteout happens when snow falls so heavily that nothing else is visible. Driving in a whiteout can cause a trucker to lose sight of the road she is driving on.

TO LEARN MORE

Books

Gordon, Nick. *Ice Road Trucker*. Minneapolis: Bellwether Media, 2013.

Gustaitis, Joseph. *Arctic Trucker*. New York: Marshall Cavendish Benchmark, 2011.

Mullins, Matt. *Trucks*. Ann Arbor, MI: Cherry Lake Publishing, 2009.

Web Sites

Visit our Web site for links about ice road truckers: childsworld.com/links

Note to Parents, Teachers, and Librarians: We routinely verify our Web links to make sure they are safe and active sites. So encourage your readers to check them out!

SELECTED BIBLIOGRAPHY

"IRT: Q&A with an Ice Road Trucking Company." *CDL Life*. CDL Life, 23 July 2013. Web. 21 June 2016.

Rowland, Hugh, and Michael Lent. *On Thin Ice: Breakdowns, Whiteouts, and Survival on the World's Deadliest Roads*. New York: Hyperion Books, 2010. Print.

Wise, Jeff. "Building Canada's Epic Ice Road." *Popular Mechanics*. Hearst Communications, 17 Dec. 2009. Web. 21 June 2016.

INDEX

ABOUT THE AUTHOR

Amy C. Rea grew up in northern Minnesota and now lives in a Minneapolis suburb with her husband, two sons, and dog. She writes frequently about traveling around Minnesota. She has also written about the lost colonists of Roanoke, the lost continent of Atlantis, and the Pony Express.